Characterizing West Africa's aspiring entrepreneurs: Who are they and which resources do they utilize?

Newton M. Campos and Till N. Folger (Authors)

Sadie Raney (Editor)

January 2018

Keywords: West Africa, Guinea-Bissau, Entrepreneurship, Effectuation, Resources.

ISBN: 9798613278510

Imprint: Independently published

Disclaimer:

The project under which this study was independently conducted was financed by the World Bank with the leadership of CESO Development Consultants in partnership with Expertise SARL, Inovisa and PB Consult.

Its inferences and findings are those of the authors and do not reflect the official position of any organization involved in the project.

1. Preface

While startup companies and the phenomenon of entrepreneurship have long been subjects of consideration in the industrialized economies of Europe and North America, the concept is no longer a novelty in most other parts of the world either. Regions such as Latin America, the Middle East and Southeast Asia have been increasingly associated with the foundation of young enterprises and a drive to innovate. Worldwide the entrepreneurial classes have been able to fill market voids with their incremental or disruptive approaches to diversifying their countries' economies into new, innovative fields.

One place in particular that has not been able to match these success stories is Western Africa. Even though the particular life circumstances here offer much room for innovation, specifically tailored to the livelihoods in the region, and for the empowerment of the local population, entrepreneurship has not taken root. Therefore, the World Bank has identified entrepreneurship as one field in which vast improvement is possible in this region and where there is significant scope for positive consequences for the populations. Not only can entrepreneurship be a tool for stimulating local markets and increasing consumer choice with more innovative products and services, the empowerment it brings to the entrepreneurs themselves is also likely to result in favorable economic and social outcomes for them and their families.

This is the exact context in which this analysis places itself, playing a part in the advancement of entrepreneurial culture in the region and strengthening the local private sector, for a better future for Western Africa and the aspiring entrepreneurs living there.

Newton M. Campos

Bissau, October 2017

2. Table of Contents

Characterizing West Africa's aspiring entrepreneurs 1

1. Preface 3
2. Table of Contents 4
3. Executive Summary 6
4. Introduction 7
5. Literature Review 9
   5.1 Country background 9
   5.2 Theory background 9
   5.3 Entrepreneurship and economic diversification 9
   5.4 Entrepreneurship in developing countries 10
   5.5 Entrepreneurship in Western Africa 11
   5.6 Social issues and gender perspective 13
   5.7 Research question 14
6. Objective, Data, and Methodology 15
   6.1 Objective of the study 15
   6.2 Data source 15
   6.3 Procedure 15
   6.4 Data specification 16
      A – Personal information 16
      B – Professional information 16
      C – Information about the new project 17
      D – Information about the existing business 17
   6.5 Methodology 17
7. Findings 18
   7.1 Basic demographic data 18
   7.2 Residence and nationality 18
   7.3 Education and languages 19
   7.4 Family background 20
   7.5 Experience and skills 21
   7.6 The startup 22
   7.7 Resources 22
   7.8 The existing business 23

8. Implications and Limitations 24
    8.1 Academic implications 24
    8.2 Implications for development work 24
    8.3 Limitations 24
    8.4 Future research 24
9. References 25

3. Executive Summary

An analysis of the profiles of applicants (here also identified as aspiring entrepreneurs) to a business plan competition in Guinea-Bissau, West Africa yielded the following findings:

1. Around 75% of aspiring entrepreneurs were male.

2. Women put a much higher emphasis on social resources, while men valued technical resources and skills more.

3. At 39%, the biggest group of applicants within the valid age range of 20 – 40 years were between 26 and 31 years old.

4. Almost 66% of applicants were residents of Bissau, the country's capital, with the rest broadly dispersed across the country and 1.3% located in other Lusophone countries or Senegal.

5. Approximately 62% of applicants had finished secondary school, vocational training, or a university course.

6. While only 15% of Guinea-Bissau's overall population speaks Portuguese, every single participant of the competition was fluent in Portuguese. Close to 99% of applicants also spoke Guinean-Bissau Creole and 60% also spoke one or more additional languages.

7. Close to 33% of applicants had a parent with an agricultural career.

8. The median applicant had 1 child and 3 persons dependent on his or her income.

9. Almost 50% of the aspiring entrepreneurs had worked in the commercial area of business or in agriculture before, making these the most common prior experiences.

10. Roughly 50% of the registered businesses applied as teams, while the other half were individual founders.

11. More than 75% of aspiring entrepreneurs listed time to dedicate themselves as one of their main resources to start a new business.

4. Introduction

With the concept of entrepreneurship on the rise as a reality in the global business world, as well as a matter of discussion and literature, the topic is also gaining momentum in the area of development cooperation. A promising tool to promote innovation, employment, and economic growth, entrepreneurial dissemination appeals to more than just industrialized nations with mature economies (Acs, Desai, & Hessels, 2008). In fact, the prospects that come with entrepreneurship are all the more relevant for developing countries caught in a struggle to improve their economic outlook. In particular, the hope to achieve economic and social progress through more inclusive growth has increasingly brought the issue on the agenda of the World Bank and other players active in the field of development cooperation.

Generally, not every country has an equally deep-rooted culture of entrepreneurship and innovation (Hayton, George, & Zahra, 2002). Additionally, even in places where such an entrepreneurial spirit is in place, an unfavorable institutional environment or lack of knowledge, skills, and financing can impede the potential of aspiring startups or prevent their formation altogether. One observed direct consequence of restricted entrepreneurial activity is limited employment creation, which usually strikes the youth most severely. This in turn often significantly affects the social and political stability of such countries.

One location with particularly pronounced difficulties for young startups are the nations of Western Africa, mostly offering small markets and low development levels for businesspeople with entrepreneurial ambitions, even though these economies are often highly focused on one specific export product and hence in dire need of diversification. A prime example for a West African economy extremely reliant on a single production good is Guinea-Bissau, where around 85% of the population is dependent on the cashew nut industry (United Nations Integrated Peacebuilding Office in Guinea-Bissau (UNIOGBIS), 2016). Especially the poor households are very likely to have no other financial income source besides cashew (Hanusch, 2016). While the number of startups globally continues to rise and the amount of available literature on the matter soars accordingly, this region has often been overlooked in the discourse.

Given these circumstances, conducting a large business plan competition offering young aspiring startup founders the opportunity to gain the necessary skills and knowledge for such an endeavor, along with professional monitoring and necessary funds, is value-adding for at least two reasons. First, it has the potential to contribute to the facilitation of business foundations by young entrepreneurs in a challenging environment.

Furthermore, such a competition also provides the chance to find out more about the aspiring entrepreneurs in Guinea-Bissau, whose ambitions are many times unattainable due to an unsupportive environment and lack of basic skills and knowledge necessary to be successful in setting up and operating a business. What characterizes these people? What resources do they intend to make use of? How do their characteristics compare to the rest of the country's population?

We used the countrywide World Bank-financed business plan competition, branded *Desafio GB*, to answer these questions. Application to Desafio GB was open to young Bissau-Guineans, aged 20 to 40, in early 2017.

From inception the program was largely influenced by the concept of *effectuation*, as introduced by Sarasvathy (2008). The term describes an approach to entrepreneurship centered on the resources the founder has at hand, out of which a business is incrementally built. Instead of having a final target in mind, the goals are to be altered flexibly throughout the process. The relevance of this concept in entrepreneurship for the West African arena, riddled with uncertainty, lies in the notion that unforeseen events in early-stage startups are a natural part of the process rather than exceptions from the norm.

Our aim with this study was to learn more about the people willing to take on such a challenge, define their profile attributes, and find out which means, in *effectuation* terms, they relied on for their endeavor.

5. Literature Review

5.1 Country background

The former Portuguese colony of Guinea-Bissau has been an independent nation since 1974. In the more than forty years following independence, the country's history has been marked by political instability, including a devastating civil war in the late 1990s. In fact, no President of the Republic has ever been able to remain in office for the entirety of his term, as government reshuffles without electoral support, often in the form of coup d'états, are a recurring reality (African Development Bank (AfDB), 2015). Political turbulence also adversely impacts the economy and the population's livelihoods. Institutions such as the United Nations (UN) and the Economic Community of West African States (ECOWAS) have stepped up efforts to end the fragility.

Despite these efforts, the country's development still has a long way to go in all traditional development measures. For example, in both the Human Development Index (UN Development Program (UNDP), 2016) and per-capita Gross Domestic Product (IndexMundi, 2014) Guinea-Bissau ranks among the bottom twenty countries globally. Despite large economic potential in areas such as fishing, mineral extraction, or tourism, the only relevant sector remains cashew growing at this time.

5.2 Theory background

The foundational theoretical groundwork in the field of entrepreneurship is generally attributed to Schumpeter (1942), who challenged the static nature of the neoclassical economic models by proposing that innovation is one of the most important drivers of disruption and progress in the economy. According to his definition, innovation is promoted by the entrepreneur, distinguishing himself from a small business owner if he engages in business activity in at least one of the following five ways (Campos, 2007):

- introducing a new good to the market;
- introducing a new production method;
- opening a new market;
- identifying a new source of supply;
- or organizing an industry in a new fashion.

While of course any aspiring non-entrepreneurial small business owner could apply to the Desafio GB program, the degree of innovation in the approach was one of the factors in deciding who would advance to the next round.

Building on Schumpeter, Sarasvathy's framework (2008) introduces another concept of relevance and interest when considering entrepreneurship as the result of a complex organizational process. Against common belief, successful entrepreneurs rarely hold an idea at the center of their entrepreneurial endeavor. Instead, the emphasis is more often on the resources the founders have at hand, along with a large amount of improvisation in the process. Such resources can be grouped into two main categories: social resources and economic resources (Campos, 2015). Effectual reasoning is especially important during the earlier stages of the startup venture and puts a strong emphasis on flexibility in dealing with unpredictable occurrences.

5.3 Entrepreneurship and economic diversification

As already mentioned, Guinea-Bissau only generates economic output in relevant amounts of a single agricultural product, namely cashew nut. With exports in services or manufactured goods being virtually non-existent, cashew is by far the most important commodity the country can sell abroad. The detrimental developmental consequences for economies entirely dependent on one or very few products have been widely discussed in the literature. Besides factors such as employment creation and output expansion, the main consequence of diversifying the economy into a broader range of sectors is reduced volatility to external shocks, one of the main growth hinderers of underdeveloped nations (International Monetary Fund (IMF), 2015).

A key problem of Guinea-Bissau lies in the fact that, as a small nation, it has no pricing power over its exports on the world market, leaving it completely vulnerable to exogenous shocks (IMF, 2015). Since the membership of the ECOWAS monetary union guarantees a remarkably stable domestic currency, many sources of volatility that comparable economies struggle with can be dodged. Regardless, possible detrimental effects include balance of payment consequences and an unstable food supply.

To avoid the potentially damaging outcomes of an undiversified economy, it is generally acknowledged that the private sector plays a key role in fostering economic diversification and serves as an engine for investments and innovation. This holds all the more true in politically unstable environments, where the public sector cannot be overly burdened with managing the economic development agenda due to limited capacities.

5.4 Entrepreneurship in developing countries

In a study of the roles and dynamics of micro and small enterprises (MSEs), Mead and Liedholm (1998) attribute this type of company a growing relevance for the context of developing economies, being a major source of employment and income. Furthermore, they find that the proportion of job creation between enterprise foundation and expansion of existing firms depends on the macro-economic outlook and on public policies, but that generally employment by small and medium enterprises (SMEs) is growing in developing countries (Mead & Liedholm, 1998).

As Dejardin (2000) points out, higher activity in Schumpeterian entrepreneurship is likely to lead to more economic growth by means of innovation. In turn, more growth can again open up more profit opportunities for potential entrepreneurs. However, he also stresses the importance of distinguishing between innovative and rent-seeking entrepreneurship, since only the former is socially productive (Dejardin, 2000). This distinction also has implications for the further progress of Desafio GB, which of course has the aim to achieve increased innovation capacity amongst the winning entrepreneurs.

Some differentiating factors between entrepreneurship in developing and industrialized countries are elaborated on by Lingelbach, De La Viña, and Asel (2005). The environment of developing countries mostly sets itself apart by the high amount of market inefficiencies, to which entrepreneurs often find counter-intuitive answers. According to the authors, new and growth-oriented enterprises have the biggest scope for causing sustainable economic growth in comparison to both established SMEs and microenterprises (Lingelbach, De La Viña, & Asel, 2005).

Lastly, Naudé (2010) makes an effort to integrate the two domains of entrepreneurship and development economics. Despite salient parallels between the two fields, they have rapidly expanded in isolation of each other. Among the conclusions he draws, the one with the most significant implications for our work is that "offering people in developing countries the choice of entrepreneurship through self-employment will be welfare-enhancing" (Naudé, 2010, p.5).

5.5 Entrepreneurship in Western Africa

Many factors that concern entrepreneurship in West Africa are very particular to the region's circumstances and might not apply in other developing regions. As Landa (1991) points out, groups of Lebanese entrepreneurs serve as middlemen with considerable significance for cross-country trade in the region. As he claims, their cultural homogeneity allows the Lebanese communities to fill many voids in the institutional framework, for example in contract enforcement (Landa, 1991). Another particularity is presented by Walther (2012), who researches the strong native and informal cross-border trade networks in the region that have a critical importance for those economies in both agriculture and commerce and lead to local entrepreneurs being very resilient and adaptable to market transformations. In this context, he therefore stresses the importance of considering the entire West African region instead of specific countries (Walther, 2012).

However, as Ekpo, Afandideh, and Udoh (2014) imply, many factors that are common throughout developing countries in general also apply in Western Africa. For instance, they encounter a strong link between the degree of economic diversification and the respective economy's stability. For the context of the ECOWAS member countries, which they study in detail, the large export dependence on a small range of primary products has resulted in lower growth figures than the African average in the years 2004 to 2009. Another relevant observation is the stressed importance the private sector has in advancing the economic situation by means of innovation and investment. Besides entrepreneurship and private-sector development, the authors name trade policy as a further factor with the potential to improve the diversification degree of West African economies (Ekpo, Afandideh, & Udoh, 2014). The recommendation of increased spending into infrastructure which facilitates the development of the private sector is what the World Bank tries to tackle with the Desafio GB project.

A comprehensive description of the outlook of entrepreneurship in the region is provided by the Global Entrepreneurship Monitor (GEM), which annually compiles attitudes of the respective populations between 18 and 64 years towards entrepreneurship in their Adult Population Survey (APS) for Burkina Faso, Ghana, Nigeria, and Senegal. For our purposes, we averaged all available scores of each country between 2013 and 2016 and then averaged these country scores. This allowed us to make statements about the region as a whole. According to the study, on average across the four nations, 71.3% saw solid opportunities to start a business in their surrounding area and as many as 84% believed they had the necessary skills and knowledge to start one. A staggering 33%, meaning every third person, in the sample were engaged in total early-stage entrepreneurial activity (TEA) at the time they were surveyed, while 22% also ran established businesses at that point.

for each country in each year, there is a remarkable homogeneity across country results with few outliers, which underlines the similarity of countries in the region.

More insights into the situation of entrepreneurship in West Africa can be gained from consulting the Ease of Doing

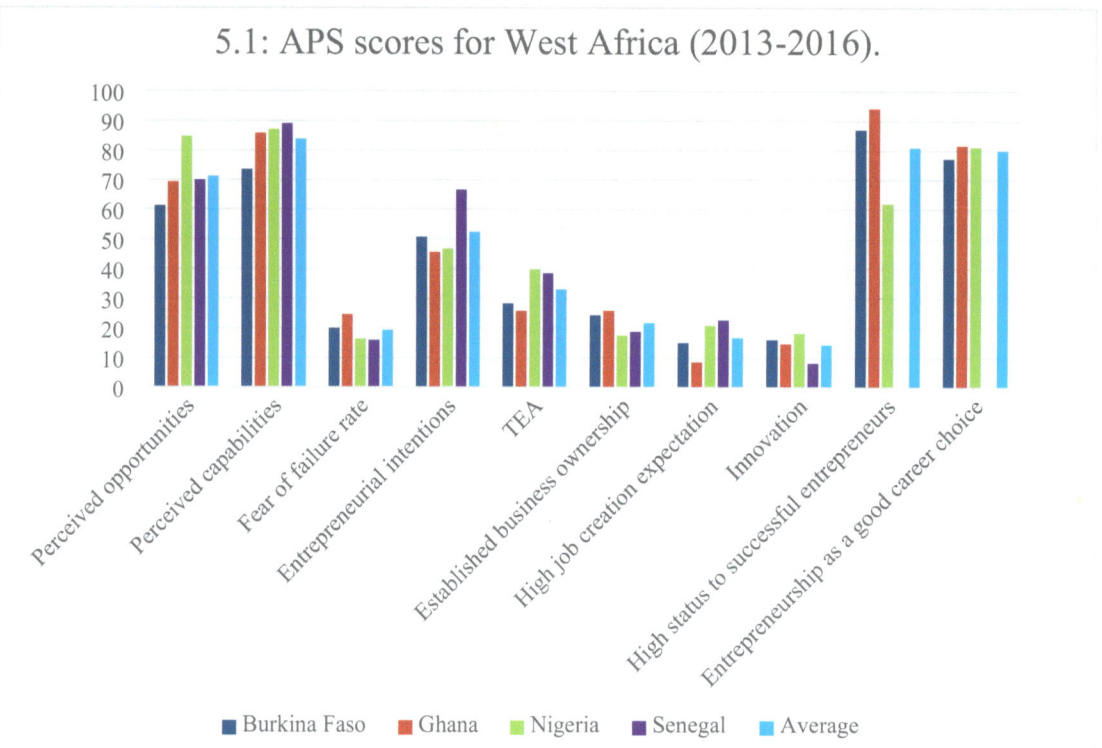

Figure 5.1: Adult Population Survey scores from the Global Entrepreneurship Monitor for West African nations, averages of available values from 2013-206. Data retrieved from http://gemconsortium.org/data/key-aps

However, only 14% of those active in TEA indicated that their approach involved some degree of innovation. This is a decisive factor in which Desafio GB tries to differentiate their participants from the apparent bulk of entrepreneurs or small business owners in the region. Lastly, the reputation of entrepreneurship in the region seems to be high, with 81% indicating that successful entrepreneurs would be rewarded with a high status and 80% that starting a business was a desirable career choice. Figure 5.1 also gives the percentages every individual country reported on average in the past years. Although the data is not complete

Business index (World Bank, 2016), which underpins the difficulties entrepreneurs face in setting up and operating businesses, both in Guinea-Bissau and in the West African region. The index, as shown in Figure 5.2, indicates how encouraging or discouraging regulations and property rights are for such activities. Despite a six-rank leap in the global ranking between 2016 and 2017, Guinea-Bissau sits at an unsatisfying 172nd place out of 190, with especially pronounced weaknesses in the areas of getting an electrical connection, enforcing contracts, obtaining credit, and, most revealing for our purposes, starting a business. While these figures manifest a somewhat below-average performance in regional comparison, the outlook in the surrounding countries is not significantly better. In all relevant indicators including the aggregate ranking, the country of choice performs similarly to the overall region.

This justifies the extrapolation of our findings beyond the nation and to the West African context. The fact that the country with the biggest relative deficit in starting a business is Guinea-Bissau only further justifies it as a valid recipient country for a project such as Desafio GB. Nigeria, West Africa's economic powerhouse, displays similar performance patterns in comparison to both the region and to Guinea-Bissau, only ranking significantly better in fields such as minority investor protection and perceived opportunities.

Another point to justify why we believe the scope of the findings is not only relevant for Guinea-Bissau itself, but also for the neighboring region is the fact that many of the ethnicities native to Guinea-Bissau reside across borders. As Table 5.1 indicates, especially the ethnic groups of Fula and Mandinga make up considerable

5.2: Ease of Doing Business in Western Africa

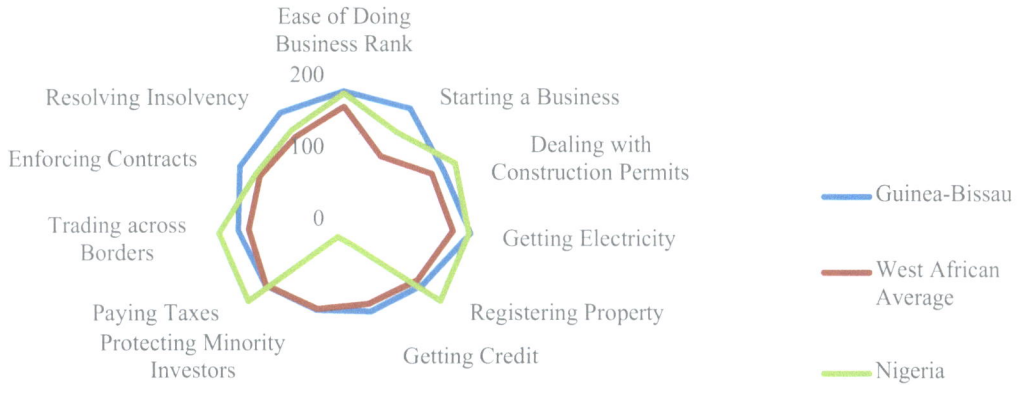

Figure 5.2: Ease of Doing Business 2017 scores of Guinea-Bissau, Nigeria, and West Africa in comparison. Data retrieved from http://www.doingbusiness.org/rankings

5.1: Fula and Mandinga ethnicities are spread widely across many West African countries.

Country	Share of Fula (%)	Share of Mandinga (%)
Guinea-Bissau	29	15
The Gambia	22	34
Guinea-Conakry	32	30
Mali	15	9
Nigeria	29	-

Table 5.1: Shares of Fula and Mandinga ethnicities among West African populations (chosen countries). Data retrieved from https://www.cia.gov/library/publications/the-world-factbook/

population shares across several West African nations.

5.6 Social issues and gender perspective

In conjunction with the prevailing high poverty levels in Guinea-Bissau, low educational attainment is further complicated by high illiteracy rates and gender discrimination. These complications remain detrimental issues to growth in the region. As of 2012, the total literacy rate was at a low 55%, with only 38% of females among the alphabetized adults (UNICEF, 2013). While the Desafio GB program does not tackle these issues directly, the empowerment it can provide is a potential positive externality that we hope to be a result of the project.

Since the setup of the business plan competition implies half of the chosen candidates at each stage must be female, it is relevant to also address the entrepreneurship domain in the region from a female perspective and the potential consequences from economic empowerment for women.

The most relevant study analyzing women entrepreneurs in Western Africa has been conducted by Otoo, Fulton, Ibro, and Lowenberg-Deboer (2010), who evaluated the roles of female street vendors in Niger and Ghana. Besides stating that women have a virtual monopoly in the street food trade, they highlight the lack of existing research in the field, alleging an underestimation of the contribution this activity has to the local economies. One of the main findings the researchers came across is that these business activities improve outcomes in health, education, and needs situations of their families. Immense overall poverty alleviation can ensue by means of three main dimensions, one being the empowerment of women who are often most prone to poverty. Additionally, the authors highlight the increased consumption of nutrition products tailored to local demand, as well as promotion of local agricultural development to spread the ingredients on which the products are based. Another finding with relevance for Desafio GB is the lack of access to financial credit, an area with great potential to improve the situation of female entrepreneurs (Otoo, Fulton, Ibro, & Lowenberg-Deboer, 2010).

5.7 Research question

As the preceding sections have shown, the entrepreneurship literature is rich and increasingly covers aspects directly related to the West African context, although not as extensively as other areas do. Besides established theoretical frameworks and findings about entrepreneurship in the developing world overall, we now have evidence specific to West Africa at our disposal. Topics covered by existing literature include cross-border social networks that support entrepreneurship in places where institutions fail to do so, the high prevalence of entrepreneurship despite the many hindrances to it, or the positive socioeconomic outcomes of successful female business ownership. The facet we still know remarkably little about are the players at the heart of the debate – the entrepreneurs themselves. This research therefore sets out to answer two very fundamental questions of characterization:

1. What is the demographic profile of a young and literate potential entrepreneur in West Africa in 2017?
2. What set of resources do these aspiring entrepreneurs claim to

possess and make use of in order to start a new business?

The following sections lay out how we attempt to tackle these questions and what the findings are.

6. Objective, Data, and Methodology

6.1 Objective of the study

With the given dataset and the apparent lack of literature at hand, the purpose of this study is clear – finding out more about the demographics of aspiring entrepreneurs in a nation classified as a "low human development" country (UNDP, 2016) and the typical set of resources they rely on for starting or improving a new business venture. Since the study is based in Guinea-Bissau, the encountered findings are expected to offer insights specifically aimed at the West African context regarding this low development level. The motivation is both to find out what characteristics describe the aspiring entrepreneurs and how they compare to the country's overall population.

The research questions are answered by quantitatively analyzing a dataset of submitted registration forms for the Desafio GB business plan competition in Guinea-Bissau. In total, more than 4,000 entries were registered for the event, received after a nationwide marketing campaign that took place for 4 months.

6.2 Data source

The study is based on data derived from the registration forms submitted for a World Bank funded business plan competition in Guinea-Bissau, named Desafio GB. The World Bank operates a host of development policies in the country under the name *Private Sector Rehabilitation and Agribusiness Development Project* (PSRADP), consisting of two components. One of these focuses on raising productivity in the already dominant cashew sector, while the other is concerned with stimulating private enterprise. Among the latter, this project is part of the subcomponent serving to support young startups, as opposed to an element engaged in improving the investment climate.

The competition takes place in several phases. Following a nationwide marketing campaign on various media channels to raise awareness about the project, registrations were opened to the general public in early 2017. Aspiring entrepreneurs were invited to apply, either online or in paper, at numerous locations across the entire country. On the application forms, they were asked to provide information about themselves and about the business idea they wanted to pursue, as described in more detail in Section 6.4.

Following this first application period 500 candidates would be chosen to receive a two-day training. As the competition advances, the groups will be incrementally decreased to 50 projects. During the interim stages, support given to the remaining entrepreneurs entails workshops and trainings. However, the final fifty remaining awardees will also receive in-kind funding, monitoring, and support in network groups until 2019. Notably, at least half of the selected projects in each round must be led by a female.

6.3 Procedure

The application period for Desafio GB took place between January and March of 2017. All of the over 4,000 entries were registered and evaluated following rigorous scoring criteria. Although most of the registration forms were submitted in paper, all entries were digitalized and combined into one dataset. The ensuing dataset is the backbone of this piece of research. While the competition's following phases are forecast to generate more data until 2019, this specific piece of research is entirely focused on the proceedings of the first phase of data collection.

6.4 Data specification

Information provided on the completed Desafio GB application forms served as the basis for the following analytical review. Registration required the applicants to provide personal information, as well as an outline of their basic business idea, on the registration form. As the forms were composed in Guinea-Bissau's official language, fluency of Portuguese was one of the requirements participants needed to fulfill. Because a local version of Portuguese Creole and several native ethnic languages are the dominant forms of communication amongst most groups in society, only 15% of Guinea-Bissau's population meet this criterion. As Portuguese language skills are usually acquired from primary school instruction and the registration had to be done in written form, the applicants can be assumed to preponderantly form part of the literate share of the country's population.

Initially, participants were asked to disclose basic information such as name, gender, birth date, nationality, as well as contact details. Applications were only considered valid if the person was between 20 and 40 years of age, held Bissau-Guinean citizenship, and indicated availability for the workshops that composed the following rounds, as well as fluency in Portuguese. If the information given was in line with the entry criteria, the residual sections were treated anonymously to make sure the person's identity would not influence the scores obtained in the following sections.

A – Personal information

The first piece of information requested in this section was if the applicant currently owned a business, had owned one in the past, or wanted to start one. It was possible to tick any amount of options, in all possible combinations. The next question concerned the level of obtained education. Possible answers were 4th, 9th, and 12th grade, vocational school, or a university degree.

With knowledge of Portuguese being a pre-condition to enter the competition, participants were then asked to state other languages they were fluent, whether Creole, European languages, or native Guinean ones. They were also asked to provide the number of visited countries and tick which continents they had been to.

The last set of information in the personal section contained questions regarding the family background. Specifically, this meant stating whether they were an only child, the oldest among siblings, or a sibling but not the oldest. Next, they were asked for specifications regarding their parents, the person or persons that had raised them, namely their professions and whether or not they owned a business. The last two questions of the section were in regard to the number of children they had, their total dependents, their monthly household earnings (with multiple options to choose from) and up to two groups or clubs they had been active in.

B – Professional information

In the middle section, participants were asked to identify their business-related competencies. Participants were asked to place a tick mark amongst the options 'private sector', 'public sector', and 'self-employment', indicating all of the ones they had worked in within the last five years. For the same time span, they were also asked to choose out of a list of six fields the ones they had worked in, or to add additional ones.

The concluding questions asked for up to three technical and social competencies, respectively, where it was possible to choose from a list or to add further options.

C – Information about the new project

Following the title specification of the project and the number and gender composition among founding members, the applicants were asked to describe their project in five open-ended questions. These were: customers or target group, main necessity of this customer group, currently existing options to respond to this necessity, a succinct description of the product or service, and an outline of the innovating or differentiating factors the product or service offered. Due to the individuality of these provided answers, these questions do not form part of the analysis.

Subsequently, the respondents were asked to state in which case they would consider the project successful, choosing one of five predefined options, and which means they possessed to meet their goals, opting for up to five out of twenty options. These means could fall into various categories – e.g. social, technical, and financial resources or other useful possessions. The next question regarded the range of impact of the project. Depending on the version of the form the possible indications were whether or not the project could have a positive impact for Guinea-Bissau or whether there was a potential impact for the city, the region, or the entire country. Lastly, the specific beneficiary area was asked to be named.

D – Information about the existing business

The last section was only required to be filled out in the case when the person had indicated that they were already operating a business. Specifications included naming the industry, the founding date, whether or not the business had formal status, the number of members and employees, main product or service on offer, and 2016 sales volume. The following question on the registration form was describing the factors about the existing business that could contribute to the success of the new project. Lastly, applicants were asked which practices from their existing business they deemed as not contributing to the company's success and would therefore avoid doing in the next entrepreneurial venture. Here, again, only the questions that were not open-ended could be analyzed.

6.5 Methodology

Given the dataset including the answers of all valid paper applications plus all entered online applications, the aim was to get a better image of what the answers to these questions were, in line with our proposed research questions. We made use of several tools in this endeavor, mostly descriptive statistics and graphs to make the findings appear more tangible at initial glance. If data was obtainable, we also tried to compare our findings with the characteristics of Guinea-Bissau's overall population.

7. Findings

Overall, we have been able to analyze all registrations to Desafio GB that were submitted online, in addition to the valid applications handed in manually, adding up to a total of 3,741 forms. Since people were allowed to hand in more than one application, the number of individual applicants is lower than this. When assessing the findings of the executed analysis, it is important to notice that all statements were made by the applicants themselves. While we believe this does not greatly decrease the validity of our findings, the possibility of biased answers resulting from self-made claims to some of the questions cannot be excluded. The number of respective answers varies from question to question. As we were not able to analyze either of the two, we disregarded both blank answers and invalid ones – e.g. choosing more options than requested.

7.1 Basic demographic data

While in each respective round of selection the gender distribution would have to be exactly equal, this did not apply for the pool of applicants before the first selection phase. In fact, out of 3,741 forms, 2,746 were handed in by men and only 899 by women, 96 being unspecified. The unspecified candidates whose score allowed them to be selected were called to confirm their gender. With the gender distribution being 73% male and only 24% female, more than three times as many project application teams were headed by men than by women. As the aspiring entrepreneurs were allowed to sign up not only by themselves, but also to represent teams, this might not be accurate for the entire candidate pool of all team members.

Conveying the information that half of the teams entering each round needed to be female-led before the registration period might have induced some teams to opt for a woman as representative instead of a man.

As mentioned before, the competition was restricted to project leaders between the ages of 20 and 40 years on the cutoff date of January 17, 2017. The overall average age of participants was 29.8 years, both for the entire population of applicants as well as for the sample in the allowed age range, showing that signups were deemed invalid for being outside the limitations on either end in almost equal dimensions. Overall, 3,614 people, or 97% of applicants were within the valid age range. We grouped this bulk into cohorts of three years each in order to get a more nuanced picture of the age distribution. The biggest cohorts were those located in the lower middle range of the distribution, with 26 to 28-year olds and 29 to 31-year olds accounting for 19.3% and 19.2% of the valid applicants, respectively. On the margins, the young groups were overrepresented, with 11% being aged 20 to 22 and only 8% between 38 and 40 years old.

7.2 Residence and nationality

The following set of questions revealed more about the places of residence and citizenship of the participants. For the residency question, the most salient point to note is the strong concentration of applicants in Guinea-Bissau's capital. Out of the 3,583 registration forms specifying the applicants' place of residence, a staggering 63% indicated living in Bissau. According to most commonly used data sources, about one in four Bissau-Guineans are estimated to reside in the capital. Even though this number is likely understated, the distribution in the total population diverges significantly from that of our applicant pool. Considering that the country's economic and political power is largely centered in Bissau can explain this finding, as the restriction to Portuguese speakers biased the sample in favor of higher socio-economic classes, which are disproportionally represented in the capital.

The following five most named cities of residence all account for between 2% and 3% of applicants. These places are Canchungo, Gabú, Catió, Bafatá, and Fulacunda. We found this result unexpected in a couple aspects. First, the presence of Fulacunda, estimated to be the 15th largest town in the nation, and second, the absence of Bissorã, which behind Bissau, Bafatá, and Gabú is the 4th most populous town and significantly closer to the capital. These unequal distributions lead to a couple questions: was the cause of these odd distributions that the target group of well-educated youngsters is overrepresented in certain places, such as Bissau, or, was the dissemination of the marketing campaign the cause of an unequally distributed turnout rate across geographical zones. The marketing campaign is a viable explanation as to why so many people from Fulacunda applied. What is more, the possibility that applicants native to the towns close to the capital might have listed Bissau instead of the actual place of residence in an attempt to increase their chances cannot be ruled out.

While 24% of applicants lived in the various residual towns and villages not previously mentioned, 47 candidates applied from residences abroad. That means that the diaspora participants accounted for 1.3% of applications. The encountered distribution among the Bissau-Guineans living abroad yields no surprises, as the bulk of these is concentrated in other Lusophone nations or in Guinea-Bissau's economically stronger neighbor of Senegal. Specifically, 40% of applications from abroad originated from Brazil, 19% from Portugal, 17% from Cape Verde, and 11% from Senegal. The residual three applications were sent in from the United Kingdom and account for 6% of the diaspora.

Registration forms furthermore asked to specify the applicant's nationality. The main aim was mostly to filter out people who were ineligible. As implied by the rules of the competition, every valid candidate had to possess a Bissau-Guinean nationality.

Notwithstanding, the option of naming an additional nationality can serve to identify some interesting findings that help to gain a better view of the applicant pool. Only 54 of the 1,645 who answered the question of whether or not they had citizenship of a second country besides Guinea-Bissau answered affirmatively. This accounts for 1.4% of all valid registrations. Amongst the dual citizens, the distribution is different from that of the diaspora, as 78% of applicants with two nationalities have one from Portugal. Close to 7% boast a Cape Verdean citizenship, while all other nations were mentioned at a maximum of two times, not exceeding the share of 3.7%.

7.3 Education and languages

Specifications regarding the attained educational level were provided by 3,650 respondents, making this question highly representative. Among these, more than a third (37%) had obtained at least some sort of professional training and almost two thirds (62%) had finished 12th grade and thereby graduated secondary school. A comparison to UNDP (2016) figures puts forward that the expected and mean attained years of schooling for a Bissau-Guinean stand at 9.2 and 2.9, respectively, supports our postulated hypothesis of an upper-class applicant pool due to the language restrictions in place.

Despite its small population, Guinea-Bissau is a multi-language society. While Portuguese, the country's official language, is only spoken by a fraction of society, Upper Guinea Creole serves as the lingua franca between native speakers of various indigenous ethnic languages. Being surrounded entirely by Francophone countries, about 5% of the population speaks French.

Given the competition's entry criterion of Portuguese mastery, not surprisingly, all of the 3,675 valid applicants that provided a specification regarding their language skills listed Portuguese. As Creole is the effective language of communication across all social and ethnic groups, 99% of the applicants indicated fluency in Creole. For a significant share (39%) this was the only mastered language besides Portuguese. A similar share of 39% spoke one or more language in addition to Creole and Portuguese. Impressively, 21% mastered two additional languages. Besides Creole, the most common languages were French and English, named by 31.2% and 20.3%, respectively. Other frequently mentioned languages were the local ethnic ones of Fula, at 8.5%, and Balanta, at 6.5%.

While European languages appear relatively more prevalent in comparison to native Guinean ones, these findings need to be treated cautiously. All native languages had to be inserted manually under 'others', whereas the aforementioned European languages could be ticked from a list. Adding to that, the participants might simply not have considered native African languages when filling in the form, leading to a potential bias in favor of French and English.

2,584 aspiring entrepreneurs had traveled abroad before applying. Out of these, 97% had been to at least one African country outside of Guinea-Bissau. Close to 16% had seen Europe and 7% a country in the Americas, while only 3.6% respectively had been to Asia or Oceania.

7.4 Family background

Out of the 3,675 answers provided to the question related to the number of siblings, significantly more than half, or 61%, answered that they were not the oldest sibling, while 32% said they were, and 6.4% had no siblings.

As the question regarding the parents' profession allowed for none, one, or two open-ended answers, this was one of the more complicated ones to analyze with accuracy. Amongst the 3,306 responses, 28% had at least one parent active in agriculture. This is significantly lower than the 82% of the country's total workforce active in this sector. Additionally, the pool of answers was spread broadly across a vast range of professional fields. The most commonly mentioned occupations were housewives, teachers, and merchants, at 15%, 11%, and 10% respectively. The bulk of residual parents were occupied in domains such as craftsmanship, public services, or security-related fields. Exactly 3,679 people answered whether or not their parents had run a business at some point. To this, 31% said yes while the remaining 69% of parents had not.

Furthermore, applicants were required to share the number of children they had (a separate question asked about the number of people depending on them). The median number of offspring was 1, while the average of 1.82 children per applicant points to the upwards skew in the distribution. The country's fertility rate stands at 5.0 (UNICEF, 2013), but in our sample only 5% reported five or higher. Considering that the average applicant was only 29.8 years old, a fertility rate below the national figure is not unexpected.

Concerning the total number of dependents relying on the applicant's income, we observed much higher figures, with an average of 4.1 persons and a median of 3 persons. However, a staggering 5.5% of respondents indicated that 11 or more people were dependent on their income.

The last specification in this category concerned household income. Almost half, or 47%, earned between XOF 30,000 and XOF 130,000 a month. According to the fixed exchange rate, this converts to €45 and €195 a month, or $48 USD to $208 USD as of February 2017[1]. A Gross National Income per capita of around $50 monthly means this group is just above the average person's yearly income. Apart from this average group, the tier earning less than $48 (29%) was larger than the tiers earning between $208 and $480 (19%), between $480 and $1,600 (4%), and $1,600 or more (1%) combined.

As another measure for social capital, the registration forms asked to list up to two clubs, associations, or other organized groups the participant was a member of. Since the named organizations were highly diverse and included religious groups, NGOs, or neighborhood organizations, amongst others, we could only study how many clubs each applicant had been active in, rather than which groups they were a member of. The average person was a part of 0.6 clubs, with 55% being a member of none at all. While 30% of aspiring entrepreneurs were part of one organization, only 14% were a part of two.

7.5 Experience and skills

As mentioned above, an early question was whether the participant currently owned a business, had owned one in the past, or would like to start one in the scope of Desafio GB. It was possible to opt for more than one choice at the same time. While 18% of applicants already owned one, only 9% had run a business in the past. The majority of 83% wanted to start a new company in the scope of the project.

Exactly 3,227 people provided answers about the sectors they had worked in before. Out of these, 22% said they had not yet worked at all. Everyone else could choose all applicable options. Less than half had been employed in the private sector, but more than a third possessed self-employment experience. Only 17% had worked exclusively in the public sector.

Regarding the experience in different business functions, 3,013 people submitted a response, of which 29% responded that they had never worked. This finding is puzzling in so far as it presents both a higher number and a higher percentage than for the same option in the preceding question. Amongst the ones that did indicate a business field, the commercial

---
[1] In the original forms, all financial data were denominated in XOF. For the stated currency conversions, exchange rates from February 24, 2017 were used: XOF 1 = $ 0.0016 and XOF 1= € 0.0015.

area was the most common choice by a considerable margin. 45% opted for this field, while the second most-named business area of operations only received 15% of the responses.

For the question about technical and professional skills 3,302 answers were collected. When asked to name up to three core competencies, nearly half of the participants (49%) named agriculture as one of them. The most progressive skill among the given options was computing, which ranked second highest at 31%.

The question regarding participants' social skills had the same set-up as the preceding one, but different answers to opt for. Here, negotiating was actually mentioned by more than half of candidates, named by 53%. The skill deemed the most useful by the selection committee, which was speaking in public, ranked second. Approximately 49% of applicants claimed to possess this competency.

7.6 The startup

About equal shares of participants aimed to start their venture as a team versus as an individual, with 52% in a group and 48% alone. Exactly 1,973 registrations specified the number of males in their team, of which in 244 cases the answer was 0. Partly due to some very high outliers, the average number here was 5.9. For the number of females, 1,837 forms contained a specification. Again, subject to some remarkable outliers, the female average amounted to 7.

Regarding the factors that define the successfulness of the project, only 7% named sustaining the family as decisive. Although this is likely to be a reason to start a business for many young entrepreneurs in the country outside the scope of the project, the upper-class candidate pool seems to be primarily driven by other motivations. Here, it is value-adding to refer to Acs et al. (2008) again, who point out that only opportunity entrepreneurship, but not necessity entrepreneurship, has a significantly positive effect on development outcomes. Therefore, observing few aspiring entrepreneurs that proclaim to be driven by necessity can be evaluated as a positive sign for Desafio GB's potential impact.

While having many satisfied employees, achieving the position of main reference in the industry, and generating a lot of profit were all named by approximately one fifth of applicants, the motivation of having many satisfied customers was by far the most popular choice, boasting 32%.

About 83% of applicants furthermore assessed the potential impact of their projects to extend to the entire country. While the rest estimated the impact to either reach their city or regional level, only 0.1% estimated the potential impact to fall below that.

Regarding the benefitting areas, the answers were widely dispersed across a broad range of possible answers with relatively unspecific descriptions. The only sectors that were named by more than one in ten aspiring entrepreneurs were food, education, as well as commerce and services. While 27% said to add value to food in the country, the other two fields boasted 14% and 13%, respectively.

7.7 Resources

For the resources the candidates intend to make use of, respondents could choose up to five out of twenty possible provided options.

Notwithstanding the large amount of possibilities, one set of five means candidates intended to make use of clearly dominated the other options. These means were using the time for personal dedication, mentioned by 65%, applying one's technical and professional abilities, stated by 46%, ambition, which 43% named, as well as physical characteristics and interpersonal skills, chosen by 38% and 37%, respectively. A common means used in industrialized countries, recognition through brands or patents, was indeed mentioned the least often, by only 2.6%.

Further interesting findings appear when comparing which resources are deemed important for each gender. The factors which have a higher importance for women by the largest margin are time to dedicate oneself, relevant contacts, and personal interest. Female candidates also found personal reputation and interpersonal skills more relevant, stressing the high importance that female respondents assigned to all sorts of resources bearing a social reference.

Men, on the other hand, were much more likely to indicate the client base or sponsor client, credit access, equipment, or geographic knowledge as important means. While the women value social resources significantly more, the same can be said for men and technical resources.

7.8 The existing business

A total of 911 candidates provided specifications regarding an existing business, as laid down in part D of section 6.4. Out of these, 790 made a statement concerning the legal status of the business. 53% reported formal business status versus 47% informal businesses, which means slightly more than half of the businesses did have a legal status.

Regarding the personnel, the average number of business partners was 8.2, with an average of 5.8 employees. Since a much higher number of business partners as compared to employees is rather unusual and both measures were subject to considerable outliers on the upper tail, the median is the more revealing metric here. For business partners, this figure stands at two, whereas the median number of employees was four.

As a last consideration, we analyzed the indicated 2016 sales volumes of the firms. This revealed a clear dominance of the small companies, with 68% of the 654 businesses having sold less than $2,400 in the year before the competition. While 16% managed to generate sales in the range above the $2,400 threshold up to twice that amount, only 3.5% of companies sold more than $16,000 in 2016.

8. Implications and Limitations

8.1 Academic implications

The aim of this study has been to present findings about the profiles of literate aspiring entrepreneurs in West Africa as well as about the resources they possess and intend to make use of for starting a business. Literature on the topic is largely lacking, therefore the findings brought by this study can contribute in this area. While the literature on entrepreneurship in the region is already scarce, it is virtually non-existent for Guinea-Bissau specifically. Therefore, the presented findings are a complete novelty in the field.

8.2 Implications for development work

The presented findings can be used by policy makers and organizers of entrepreneurship competitions similar to Desafio GB as they indicate clearly the characteristics to which such a program appeals. Drawing on these findings and potentially specified targets for comparable future endeavors, developers of similar programs can hence define the competition design accordingly. In this context, it is important to bear in mind the consequences that entry limitations can have on the characteristics of the ensuing candidate pool. Beyond that, the presented findings can also add value for all other sorts of development work in entrepreneurship in Western Africa.

8.3 Limitations

One limitation inherent to the dataset this work is based on is that not every registration necessarily represents exactly one person, which might add a small margin of error to the results. Additionally, the unequal response rate to the questions might indicate some bias. Additionally, the sample could have been biased by the way the marketing campaign was designed. Although the campaign covered a broad range of media outlets and geographical locations in the country, it is improbable that they were able to reach every potential applicant equally. Lastly, the geographical factor presents a potential limitation. While, as outlined before, the authors expect the findings to be valid for the entire context of West Africa, extrapolations beyond this region are not recommended.

8.4 Future research

A number of questions valuable to tackle in future research come to mind that either fall out of the scope of this research or are not feasible at this early stage of the Desafio GB program. One question would certainly be to what extent the encountered characteristics generated positive and negative outcomes for the business. Another value-adding area of research could consider the profiles of entrepreneurs in a different socioeconomic segment, perhaps in a comparable program where language restrictions do not exclude such a big part of society as in our case.

9. References

Acs, Z. J.; Desai, S.; & Hessels, J., 2008. Entrepreneurship, economic development and institutions. *Small Business Economics, 31*, 219-234. Doi: 10.1007/s11187-008-9135-9.

African Development Bank (AfDB), 2015. Guinea-Bissau 2015-2019 Country Strategy Paper.

Campos, N. M., 2010. Entrepreneurship in Socioeconomic and Political Instability. ENEO 2010.

Campos, N. M., 2015. The Myth of the Idea and the Upsidedown Startup: How Assumption-based Entrepreneurship has lost ground to Resource-based Entrepreneurship. Charleston, SC: CreateSpace Independent Publishing Platform.

Central Intelligence Agency (CIA), 2017. The World Factbook. Retrieved from https://www.cia.gov/library/publications/the-world-factbook/

Dejardin, M., 2000. Entrepreneurship and Economic Growth – an Obvious Conjunction? An Introductive Survey to Specific Topics. Indiana University Institute for Development Strategies.

Ekpo, A. H.; Afandigeh, U. J.; Udoh, E. A., 2014. Private Sector Development and Economic Diversification: Evidence from West African States. In D. Seck (ed.), *Advanced in African Economic, Social and Political Development*. Switzerland: Springer International Publishing.

Global Entrepreneurship Monitor (GEM), 2017. *Entrepreneurial Behaviour and Attitudes*. Retrieved from http://www.gemconsortium.org/data

Hanusch, M., 2016. Guinea-Bissau and the cashew economy. *Macroeconomics & Fiscal Management Practice Notes, 11*, 1-8. Washington DC: World Bank Group.

Hayton, J. C.; George, G.; & Zahra, S. A., 2002. National Culture and Entrepreneurship: A Review of Behavioral Research. *Entrepreneurship Theory and Practice, 26 (4)*, 33-52.

IndexMundi. (January 1, 2014). Country comparison: GDP per capita (PPP). Retrieved from https://www.indexmundi.com/g/r.aspx?v=67

International Monetary Fund (IMF), 2015. Guinea-Bissau Selected Issues. IMF Country Report No. 15/195.

Landa, J. T., 1991. Culture and Entrepreneurship in Less-Developed Countries: Ethnic Trading Networks as Economic Organizations. In B. Berger (ed.), *The Culture of Entrepreneurship*. San Francisco, California: ICS Press.

Lingelbach, D.C.; De La Vina, L.; Asel, P., 2005. What's Distinctive about Growth-Oriented Entrepreneurship in Developing Countries? UTSA College of Business Center for Global Entrepreneurship Working Paper No. 1. Retrieved from https://papers.ssrn.com/sol3/papers.cfm?abstract_id=742605

Mead, D. C.; Liedholm, C., 1998. The Dynamics of Micro and Small Enterprises in Developing Countries. *World Development, 26*(1), 61-74.

Naudé, W., 2010. Entrepreneurship, developing countries, and development economics: new approaches and insights. *Small Business Economics, 34*, 1-12. doi: 10.1007/s1187-009-9198-2.

Otoo, M.; Fulton, J.; Ibro, G.; Lowenberg-Deboer, J., 2011. Women Entrepreneurship in West Africa: The Cowpea Street Food Sector in Niger and Ghana. *Journal of Developmental Entrepreneurship, 16*(1), 37-63. doi: 10.1142/S1084946711001732.

Sarasvathy, S. D., 2008. Effectuation: Elements of Entrepreneurial Expertise. Edward Elgar Pub. Northampton, MA, USA.

Schumpeter, J. A., 1942. *Capitalism, Socialism & Democracy*. London, UK / New York City: Routledge.

UNICEF, 2013. *At a glance: Guinea-Bissau*. Retrieved from https://www.unicef.org/infobycountry/guineabissau_statistics.html

United Nations Development Program (UNDP), 2016. Human Development 2016. Retrieved from http://report.hdr.undp.org/

United Nations Integrated Peacebuilding Office in Guinea-Bissau (UNIOGBIS). (April 11, 2016). Cashew nut central to Guinea-Bissau economy: a blessing or a curse? Retrieved from https://uniogbis.unmissions.org/en/cashew-nut-central-guinea-bissau-economy-blessing-or-curse

Walther, O., 2012. Traders, agricultural entrepreneurs and the development of cross-border regions in West Africa.Entrepreneurship & Reguianl development, 24(3-4), 123-141. doi: 10..1080/08985626.2012.670909.

World Bank (October 25, 2016). Doing Business 2017. Retrieved from http://www.doingbusiness.org/reports/global-reports/doing-business-2017

www.ingramcontent.com/pod-product-compliance
Lightning Source LLC
Chambersburg PA
CBHW051941210526
45473CB00006B/2340